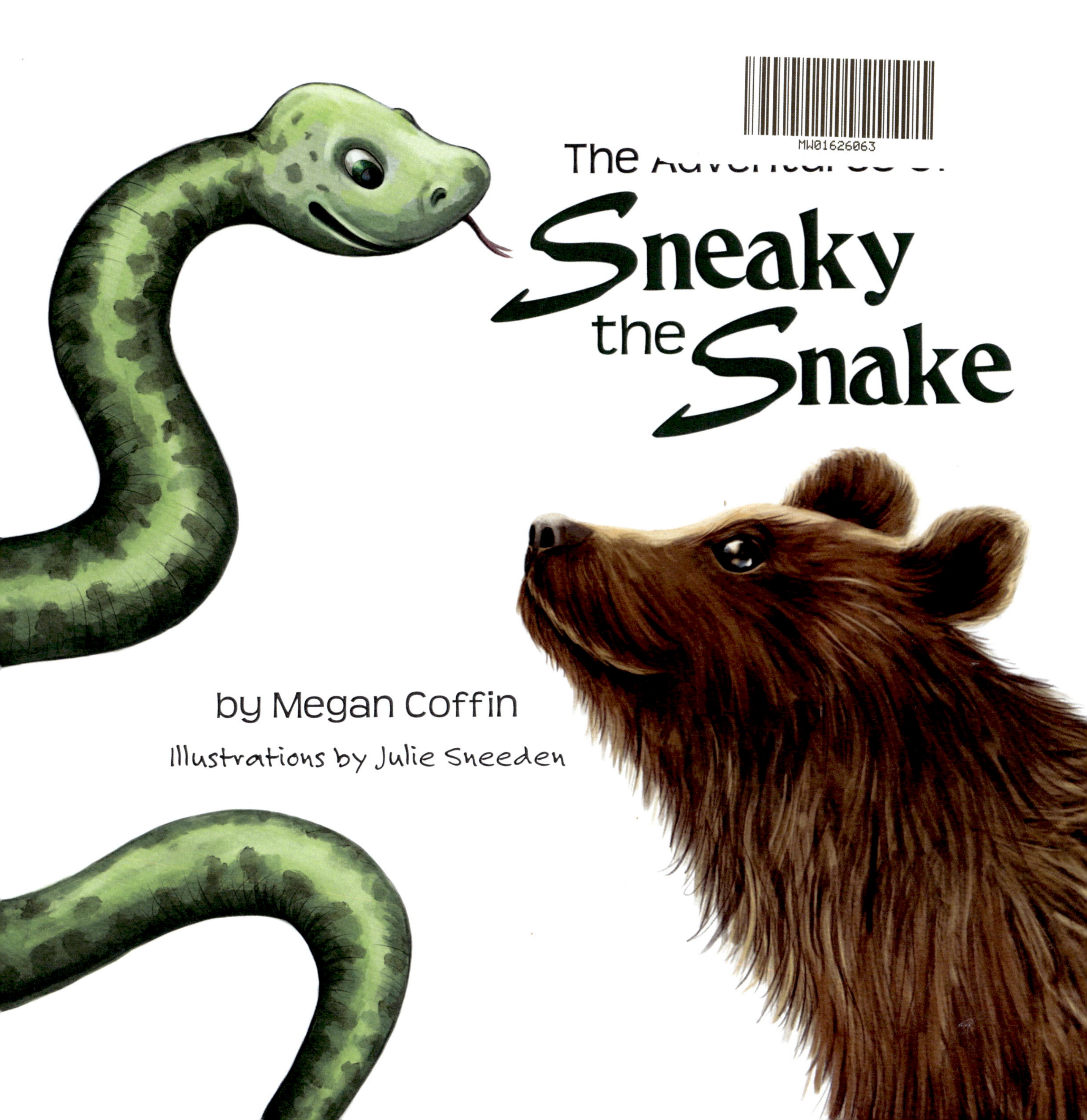

MW01626063
The Adventures of
Sneaky the Snake
by Megan Coffin
Illustrations by Julie Sneeden

Published and written by Megan Coffin

Copyright © 2022 Megan Coffin

Illustrated by Julie Sneeden

All Rights Reserved. No part of this publication may be reproduced, stored in a retrieval system, or transmitted, in any form or in any means – by electronic, mechanical, photocopying, recording or otherwise – without prior written permission of the author.

All rights reserved worldwide

ISBN: 978-1-7781921-0-4

www.theadventuresofsneakysnake.com

Dedicated to...

For Dad, who provided me with the inspiration for this story.
Thank you for creating my favorite memory.

This is a story about a *snake*; his name is *Sneaky*, *Sneaky* the *Snake*. *Sneaky* lived in a large rock pile at the edge of Farmer Brown's field. Every morning *Sneaky* would crawl out from under his rock pile and slither up on top of the rocks to soak up the early morning sun.

This particular morning Sneaky was interrupted by a loud noise. Sneaky lifted his head to look around and saw Farmer Brown coming down the field, plowing the ground behind him. Sneaky knew right then and there that the Farmer was expanding his field, and this was no longer the place to live.

Early the next morning, Sneaky started across the newly plowed field. "Brrr" Sneaky said. The earth was cold and damp on Sneaky's belly.

After a short while, *Sneaky* was in the farmyard. Where he saw Harry Horse, Ricky Rat and many other of his farmyard friends. It was loud and crowded. *Sneaky* said to himself ,This is NOT where I would like to live".

Sneaky continued to slither across Farmer Brown's farm where he came to a fence. He knew he was far from his rock pile where he once called home. He felt sad but crawled under the fence and slithered toward the forest.

After some time, *Sneaky* came to a brook with no where to cross. He continued up stream where he found a large mound of tree branches piled up that stretched across the brook. "I can cross here!" *Sneaky* said happily and started crossing over the large mound of sticks which seemed to slow down the water in the brook.

He was startled as he heard a large slapping sound and a voice call out, "Hey! What are you doing crossing over my dam!" a little black head peered out of the water. "Who are you?" *Sneaky* said that's a bad word! "My name is Bucky, and you are on my home, I am a beaver and my home is called a dam". "My name is a *Sneaky*, Sneaky the Snake, pleasure to meet you! I am on my way to the Forest to find a new home, it got too noisy by the rock pile over on the other side of Farmer Brown's field".

"I know the perfect place for you" said Bucky, "follow my path of broken trees and you will come to a great big meadow. If you look over at the far end of the meadow, you will see a great big tree, with great big branches. I think it will make a great new home for you. *Sneaky* thanked Bucky for all his help and knew he found a new Forest friend.

Sneaky started travelling up Bucky's path. Sneaky slithered easily along the path because Bucky would cut down the trees with his teeth and drag them back to build his Dam. Sneaky arrived at the edge of the meadow where he could see a large tree, just like Bucky said.

He moved very quickly through the tall grass of the meadow towards the large tree. When he arrived at the tree, he looked up....and up....and up, and saw exactly where he wanted to live, a large branch that stretched out over the meadow, just like a large arm.

Sneaky slithered up the large tree trunk, up, up, and up he went until he came to the branch where he would call his new home, it was so large it would fit FIVE snakes.

Sneaky was getting snug in his new home when the great big tree started to shake! Nearly shaking *Sneaky* off his branch.

Sneaky looked all around and could not see what is causing such a commotion in his tree, then he looked down at the bottom of the tree and saw a large animal standing tall scratching his back on the tree trunk. "Hey! What are you doing down there? You are going to shake me right off my branch!" Sneaky yelled. "Oh, I am sorry! I didn't see you up there!" Sneaky came closer, it was A BEAR! Sneaky was scared of Bears.

"My name is a Bernie Bear, don't be scared of me, I won't hurt you! I have been coming to this tree for back scratches since I was a little bear cub." said Bernie. "My name is *Sneaky* the *Snake*, I just moved here".

Bernie was very excited to meet a new friend "I just came out of hibernation; I rested all winter; I am very itchy and very hungry! Would you like to come with me, and I can show you around the forest?" *Sneaky* was excited to already meet a new forest friend and welcomed the opportunity to go on a new adventure with Bernie Bear.

The two started down the path Bucky built, to search for berries and visited the local fishing hole where Bernie and his family would fish every Spring and Summer. *Sneaky* stretched out on a large rock pile warmed by the sun and watched Bernie try to catch his lunch. The two spent the rest of the day exploring around *Sneaky's* new home.

The sun was sinking below the trees, it was getting late. The two friends returned to *Sneaky's* large tree in the meadow and said their goodbyes. "I will see you tomorrow and we will explore more, together". Bernie said as he was walking away.

Sneaky was happy, he took a moment and looked around as the sun was setting. He was sad and would miss his friends from the farm but was excited to see what new friends he would find in the Forest. He stretched out, smiled and quickly went to sssssssssssleep.